Banks

Margaret Hall

Heinemann Library
Chicago, Illinois

Customer Service 888-454-2279
Visit our website at www.heinemannlibrary.com

Designed by Kimberly R. Miracle and Cavedweller Studio
Photo Research by Tracy Cummins and Heather Mauldin
Printed by Leo Printing Company

12 11 10 09 08
10 9 8 7 6 5 4 3 2

New edition ISBNS: 978-1-4034-9814-4 (hardcover)
                    978-1-4034-9819-9 (paperback)

Library of Congress Cataloging-in-Publication Data
Hall, Margaret, 1947-
  Banks / Margaret Hall.
     p. cm. -- (Earning, saving, spending)
  Originally published: c2000.
  Includes bibliographical references and index.
  ISBN 978-1-57572-231-3 (hc) -- ISBN 978-1-58810-337-6 (pb)
  1. Banks and banking--Juvenile literature. [1. Banks and banking.] I.
Title. II. Series: Hall, Margaret, 1947- Earning, saving, spending.
  HG1609.H35 2008
  332.1--dc22
                        2007015147

Acknowledgments
The author and publishers are grateful to the following for permission to reproduce
copyright material: Corbis **pp. 4** (Royalty free), **9** (Comstock), **15** (James Leynse), **22**
(Marianna Day Massey/ZUMA), **23** (Owaki/Kulla); Getty Images **pp. 6** (Andrew Sacks),
10 (Royalty free), **12** (Royalty free), **18** (Royalty free), **19** (Royalty free), **20** (Royalty free),
21 (Zia Soleil), **27** (Royalty free), **29** (Kevin Cooley); Heinemann Raintree **p. 26** (David
Rigg); istockphoto **p. 11** (Sean Locke); Jupiter Images **p. 8** (Comstock Images); Alan
Klehr **p. 17**; PhotoEdit **pp. 5** (Michael Newman), **7** (Tony Freeman), **13** (Robert Brenner),
14 (Michelle D. Bridwell); Shutterstock **pp. 16** (Alexei Daniline), **24** (Amy Waltersr), **25**
(Stephen Coburn).

Cover photographs reproduced with permission of Gary Buss/Getty Images and Royalty
free/ Getty Images (piggybank).

Contents

Some words are shown in bold, **like this**. You can find out what they mean by looking in the glossary.

What Is a Bank?

A bank is a business that offers services that help people use and save money. When someone keeps money in a bank, the bank takes care of it. But, the person can use his or her money at any time.

People keep money in banks because banks are safe.

Banks might look different, but they all offer services to help people use money.

There are different types and sizes of banks. A bank can be big enough to fill a whole building. A bank can also be tucked into the corner of another business, such as a supermarket. But, all banks offer services that help people with money.

A Safe Place for Money

A bank puts money and other valuable things in a special, safe room called a **vault**. A vault has strong locks and is fireproof. Banks have guards, locks, and alarms. It is hard for anyone to steal from a bank.

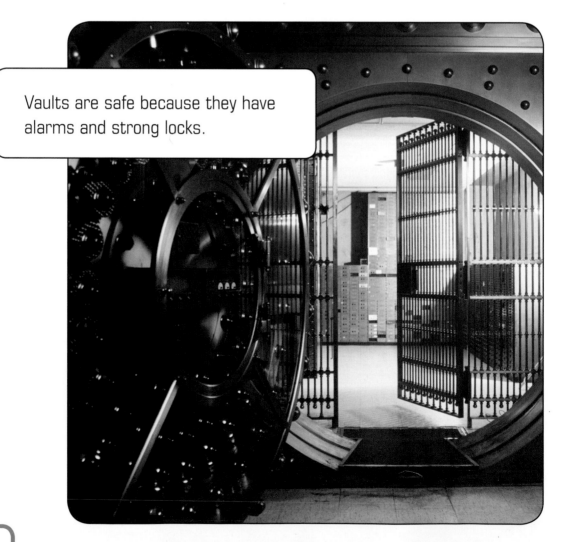

Vaults are safe because they have alarms and strong locks.

The **government** helps keep money in a bank safe, too. The government has rules about what banks can and cannot do with the money people put there. Also, if money is stolen from a bank, the government will give the bank money so that people do not lose the money they put in the bank.

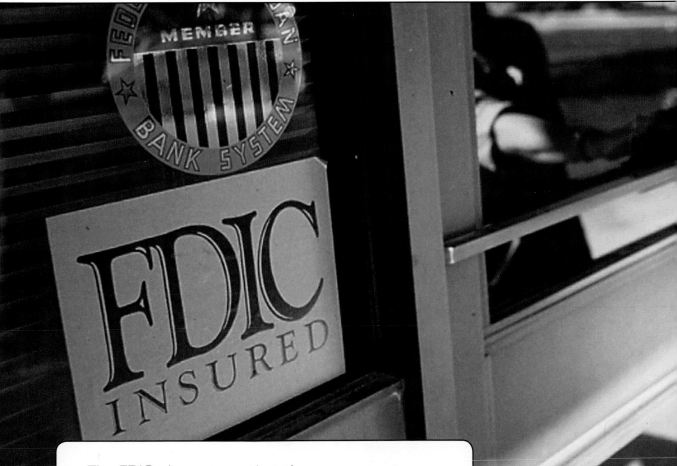

The FDIC sign means that the government watches over the bank. FDIC means "Federal **Deposit Insurance** Corporation."

Bank Services

A bank is a place to save money. Banks hold money for people, and they let people have their money when it is needed. A bank is a place to borrow money, too. When people need money, a bank can help them.

Banks use the money people keep there to help other people and businesses.

Important papers and expensive jewelry are some of the items people put in safe-deposit boxes.

Banks also have safe-deposit boxes that are kept in the **vault**. People can keep important papers and valuable items, like jewelry, in them. Only the person who has the special key for the box can open it.

Checking Accounts

A **checking account** is a bank service that lets people use money without having to carry **cash**. To open a checking account, a person gives some money to the bank. This is called making a **deposit**.

When using checks to pay for items, people must know exactly how much money they have in their checking accounts.

To pay using a check, account owners must write in the date, whom to pay, how much to pay them, and then sign their own name on the check.

The bank gives the person a **checkbook** with checks in it. A check is like a note telling the bank to pay some of the person's money to someone else. People can deposit money into their checking account whenever they want. They can also take money out of their account. This is called making a **withdrawal**. Deposits and withdrawals are types of **transactions**.

Savings Accounts

People open **savings accounts** to help them save for the future. Usually, money in a savings account is money they do not plan to use right away. People can **deposit** or **withdraw** money from their savings accounts whenever they want.

Most banks offer different kinds of savings accounts to help their customers save money for the future.

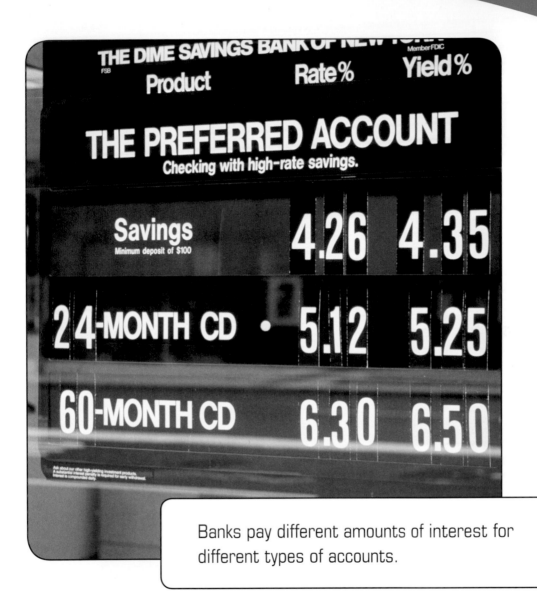

Product	Rate%	Yield%

THE DIME SAVINGS BANK OF NEW YORK
FSB
Member FDIC

THE PREFERRED ACCOUNT
Checking with high-rate savings.

Product	Rate%	Yield%
Savings Minimum deposit of $100	4.26	4.35
24-MONTH CD ·	5.12	5.25
60-MONTH CD	6.30	6.50

Ask about our other high-yielding investment products.
A substantial interest penalty is required for early withdrawal.
Interest is compounded daily.

Banks pay different amounts of interest for different types of accounts.

The bank uses the money in savings accounts to run its business. In return, the bank pays savings accounts customers a special **fee** called **interest**. The interest is added to the money in the account. The longer money stays in the account, the more interest it earns.

Loans

Most people do not have enough money to pay for expensive items like a house or car all at once. They can borrow the money they need from a bank. The borrowed money is called a **loan**.

Most cars cost more money than people can pay at one time.

Loans must be paid back to the bank over a set period of time. In exchange for the service of borrowing a lot of money, the person must also pay the bank **interest**. The interest is added to the amount borrowed, so people end up paying back more money than they borrowed.

Banks make money by charging interest on loans.

Bank Cards

Banks offer special cards to their customers called **bank cards**. **Credit cards** are a type of bank card that lets people buy things now and pay for them later. Using credit cards is like getting a small **loan**. If the money is not paid back right away, the bank charges **interest**.

The interest rate people must pay for using a credit card is much higher than for a small loan.

Debit cards look like credit cards, but they work like checks.

Debit cards are bank cards that work like **checks**. When people pay for things with debit cards, the money really comes from their **checking accounts**. Businesses must pay banks a **fee** every time someone pays them with a credit card or debit card. Banks make money from these fees and from the interest they charge on credit cards.

Working with Customers

Many people work in a bank. Some have jobs helping bank customers. A bank teller works behind the counter at a bank. Customers can make **withdrawals** and **deposit** money in their accounts with the teller's help. Tellers help make all kinds of **transactions**.

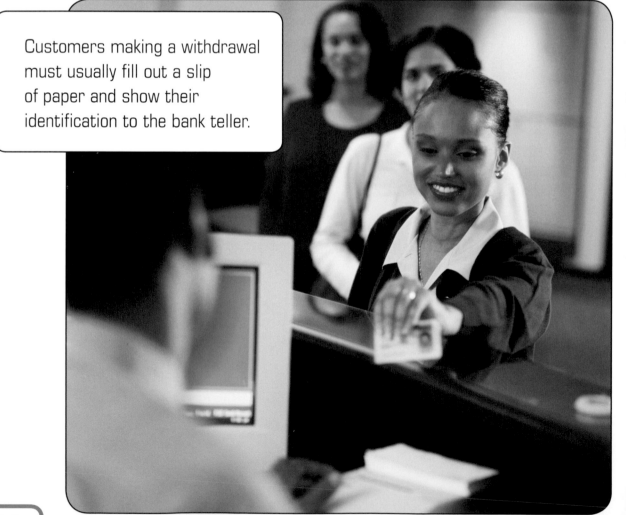

Customers making a withdrawal must usually fill out a slip of paper and show their identification to the bank teller.

Loan officers try to get the best loans for their customers.

Bank officers help to open new accounts. They can also answer questions and give advice about money. **Loan** officers work with people who want to borrow money from the bank. They ask questions and help to fill out the papers needed to get the best loan for the customer.

Working Behind the Scenes

Some bank workers do not work directly with customers. Accountants keep track of the money kept in accounts at the bank. They pay the bank's bills and keep records about the bank's business. Computer workers run the bank's computers. Computers help keep track of money in the accounts and figure out how much **interest** should be charged or paid to customers.

Accountants make sure that the bank has enough money to stay in business.

Customer service representatives do some of the same jobs bank tellers do. However, they help people who choose to make **transactions** over the phone. They also help people who call the bank with questions about their accounts. Bank guards help keep the bank safe. There are many other workers needed to run a bank. In some way, every worker's job helps the bank to offer services to its customers.

Customer service representatives help customers who choose to do business by phone.

Banking Without a Bank

Even when the bank is closed, people can use its services. They can do this with machines called **Automated Teller Machines**, or **ATMs**. ATMs are found in many places, and they can be used at any time.

ATMs are found in many places, such as banks, malls, and supermarkets.

ATMs do many things, including taking **deposits** and giving **cash**.

ATMs are hooked up to the bank's computers. So, they can do many of the things a bank teller does. Many banks also offer services on the **Internet**. People can use the Internet to make **transactions**, see how much money is in their accounts, or use their checking account to pay their bills. This is called banking **online**.

23

How an ATM Works

An **ATM** works with a **credit card** or **debit card**. When the card is put into the ATM, the bank's computer reads a code that is in a strip on the back of the card.

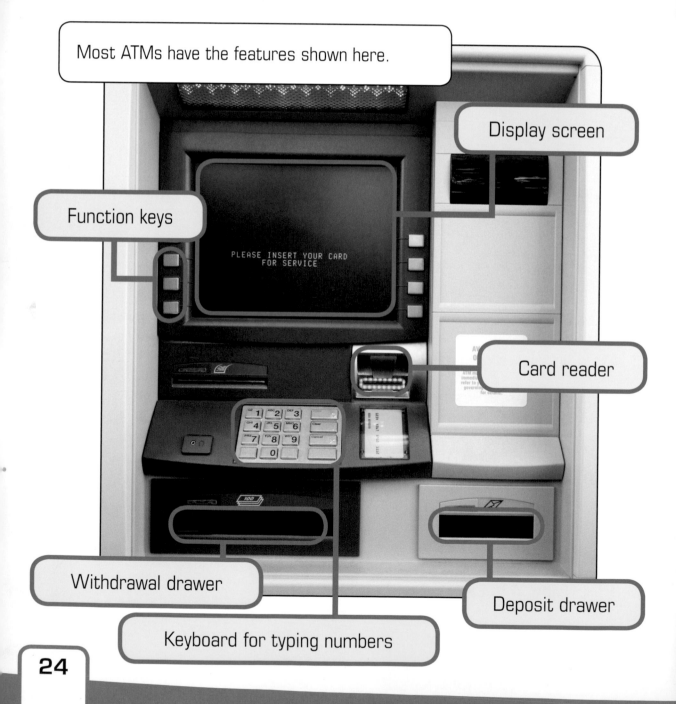

Most ATMs have the features shown here.

Display screen

Function keys

PLEASE INSERT YOUR CARD FOR SERVICE

Card reader

Withdrawal drawer

Deposit drawer

Keyboard for typing numbers

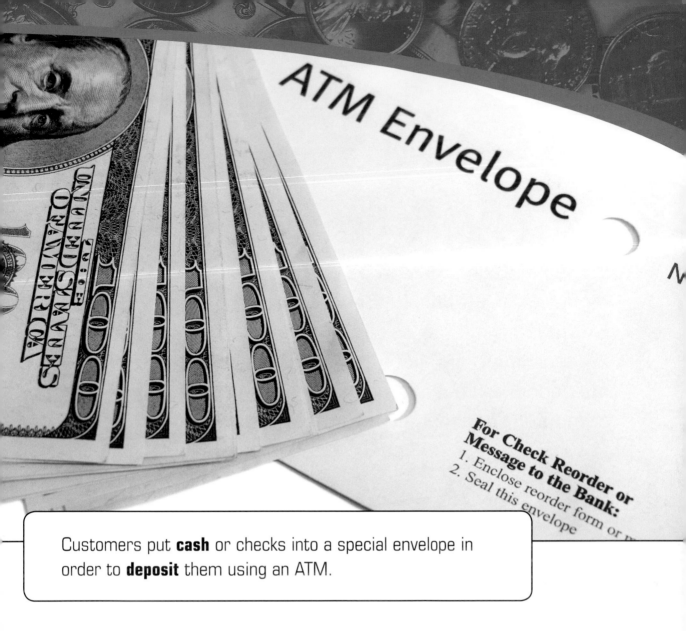

ATM Envelope

For Check Reorder or
Message to the Bank:
1. Enclose reorder form or p
2. Seal this envelope

Customers put **cash** or checks into a special envelope in
order to **deposit** them using an ATM.

Then the ATM display screen asks the customer to type in
a secret number called a **personal identification number
(PIN)**. The PIN is a way to keep money in an account safe.

Next, the ATM asks the customer questions about the
transaction he or she wants to make. The customer
chooses answers to the questions by pushing buttons or
touching the display screen. The bank will keep track of the
transaction. The ATM prints a **receipt** for the customer.

Keeping Track of Money

Banks keep careful records to show what happens to money. When someone **deposits** money, the amount is entered into the bank's computers. The computer prints out a **deposit slip** that tells how much money went into the account. If a customer makes a **withdrawal**, the computer prints out a **withdrawal slip**.

Customers also fill in withdrawal or deposit slips to make those **transactions**.

Account number

Name

WITHDRAWAL

Date

DEPOSIT

Amount of deposit

When people use ATMs, they get a receipt.

The bank's computers keep track of every transaction. Even when customers use ATMs they get a **receipt** as a record of the transaction. Also, once every month, customers get a **bank statement** in the mail. The statement describes everything that happened with the customer's accounts in that month.

Bank Statements

Customers should read their **bank statements** carefully to make sure that every **transaction** has been recorded. If there is a mistake, the bank should be told right away. Statements usually come through the mail.

A bank statement like this one shows everything that happened with the customer's account in one month.

First Provident Bank
226 North Canal Street, Draper, Utah 84020

ROBERT J SMITH
341 BANGERTER HWY
BLUFFDALE UT 84065-1421

MONTHLY CLIENT UPDATE	
Statement Date:	04/03/08
Page 1 of 2	
Account Number	12345678

Account owner's name

Beginning and ending date for statement

Checking account number

CHECKING STATEMENT

Statement Cycle:	30 days	Service Charge:		
Begining Balance:	1503.76			
Deposits/ Misc Credits:	1162.14	Average Balance:	1298.4	
Withdrawals/Misc Debits:	1304.10	Enclosures:		
Ending Balance:	1361.82			

Beginning total

Money left in account

TRANSACTION DETAILS

Date	Description	Withdrawals	Deposits	Balance
				1403.76
				1340.58
02/09/08	ATM WITHDRAWAL/TRANS 12345	100.00		1313.08
02/10/08	CHECK PAID #979	63.20		1663.08
02/15/08	POS PURCHASE CHECK/TRANS	27.50	350.00	1569.93
02/20/08	DDA DEPOSIT			549.68
02/23/08	POS PUR/PIN CHK/TRANS 12345	93.15		1361.82
02/28/08	CHECK PAID # 980	1020.25	812.14	
03/02/08	CASH DEPOSIT			

Withdrawal

Deposit

CHECKS POSTED

Date	Check No.	Amount
		63.20
		1020.25
02/10/08	0979	
02/28/08	0980	

Check payment

ATM-DEBIT CARD SUMMARY

Date	Type	Amount	Location
			ATM WITHDRAWAL
			BLUE SPRING MALL BLUFFDALE UT
02/09/08	WTH	100.00	POS PURCHASE CHECK/ EFT TRANS
			AMOCO OIL SOUTH RIVER UT
02/15/08	WTH	27.50	POS PUR/PIN CHK/ EFT TRANS
02/23/08	WTH	93.15	CVS SUPERMARKET BLUFFDALE UT

TOTAL WITHDRAWALS: TOTAL DEPOSITS AND ENDING BALANCE

More and more people are choosing to do their banking online.

Some customers bank **online**. They use the **Internet** to look at their statement. They have to sign into their account using a special **password**. Bank statements are important because they help customers keep track of their money.

Glossary

Automated Teller Machine (ATM) machine that lets people use bank services without seeing a bank teller

bank card plastic card given by a bank to a customer that can be used to buy things instead of using cash

bank statement record of what happens to the money a person keeps in a bank

cash coins and paper money

checkbook booklet of checks

checking account service offered by a bank that lets people use their money without carrying cash

credit card thin, plastic bank card that lets someone buy something and pay for it later

debit card thin, plastic bank card, used instead of a check, that lets someone pay for something using money from their checking account

deposit money put into a bank account; or, to put money into a bank account

deposit slip record of money that is deposited into a bank account; or, slip a person fills out to make a deposit

fee money charged for a service

government leadership of a country, state, or town

insurance protection and safety against loss

interest money charged for borrowing money; or, money paid to people for letting the bank use their money to run its business

Internet network of computers around the world through which information is shared

loan money someone borrows

online connected to the Internet

password secret code made from letters and/or numbers

personal identification number (PIN) secret number only the account owner knows and uses at ATMs to deposit and withdraw money from accounts

receipt record showing the amount of a transaction or how much someone spent

savings account service offered by a bank for saving money

transaction business deal done with a bank

vault room in a bank for keeping money and valuable things safe

withdrawal money taken out of a checking or savings account

withdrawal slip record of money that is taken out of a bank account; or, slip a person fills out to make a withdrawal

Find Out More

Allman, Barbara. *Banking.* Minneapolis, MN: Lerner Publications, 2006.

Bagley, Katie. *Bank Tellers.* Bloomington, MN: Capstone Press, 2001.

Rau, Dana Meachen. *What Is a Bank?* Milwaukee, WI: Gareth Stevens, 2006.

To learn more about money in the United States, visit the United States Department of the Treasury Education website at: http://www.ustreas.gov/education/

Index